Prairie Dogs

ANIMAL PREY

SANDRA MARKLE

Lerner Publications Company / Minneapolis

THE ANIMAL WORLD
IS FULL OF
PREY.

Prey are the animals that predators eat. Predators must find, catch, kill, and eat other animals in order to survive. But prey animals aren't always easy to catch or kill. Some have eyes on the sides of their heads to let them see predators coming from all directions. Some are colored to blend in and hide. Some prey are built to run, leap, fly, or swim fast to get away. And still others sting, bite, or use chemicals to keep predators away. *The prairies (grasslands) of North America and Mexico are home to black-tailed prairie dogs, who live in large groups for safety.*

It's an early May morning on the South Dakota prairie. One by one, the members of this black-tailed prairie dog group come out from different entrances to their underground burrow. The biggest adults are about the size of a small house cat. The yearlings, last year's offspring, are only a little smaller than the adults.

Before they move away from the safety of their burrows, the prairie dogs look around for predators, such as coyotes or bobcats, that might be lurking nearby. Prairie dogs have big eyes set wide on their heads. This helps them see about two-thirds of the way around themselves at one glance.

Each prairie dog group claims about 1 acre (about 0.5 hectare) of prairie. Other groups' territories lie close by. Together these territories form a prairie dog colony, or town. The colonies usually cover a few miles (kilometers) and are home to about one hundred to two hundred prairie dogs. Some towns have thousands of prairie dogs.

While they eat, prairie dogs prune the prairie grasses. This helps new leaves to grow. The young shoots are soft and nutritious. Short grass also makes it easier for the colony to watch for predators. This female, the older of two females in the colony, sits up tall to look for predators while she eats.

It has rained hard during the night. A domed mound of earth keeps most water out of the animals' burrow. But the rain washed away some of the dirt. So the colony's one adult male goes to work. He digs with his front paws and kicks dirt backward with his back paws to build up the mound again. Then he packs the dirt by lying on it and patting it down with his nose.

Near the edge of the group's territory, a young female meets another female. The two of them greet each other by putting their mouths close together and touching tongues. This way the animals check each other to see if either is an intruder.

Individual groups don't welcome prairie dogs from other colonies. These visitors might eat some of their food supply. So when the young female realizes the other female is not from her group, she makes a loud chattering noise. When the stranger doesn't immediately leave, the young female attacks. The pair wrestles. Each struggles to nip the other's cheeks, sides, or legs.

Chirk! Chirk! Chirk! Sharp barks mean that the prairie dog sees a predator. The speed and tone of the barks mean that the enemy is a golden eagle. Other prairie dogs repeat the warning. The females forget their fight and run for their group's closest burrow entrance.

The golden eagle swoops down until it's just above the waving sea of prairie grass. Its shiny, black eyes scan the fleeing swarm of prairie dogs. The eagle looks for a prairie dog that's slower and weaker—one it can catch in its sharp talons (claws).

Every group of prairie dogs has many burrow entrances. But none of the prairie dogs immediately ducks underground. If every animal was in its burrow, none of the prairie dogs would know what the eagle was doing. It could continue to circle, waiting to strike the first prairie dog to pop out of its burrow.

When the hunter swoops toward the group's two adult females and a yearling, they dive in their burrows. The younger female and yearling scurry all the way down to a chamber that's nearly 15 feet (about 4.5 meters) underground. The older female ducks into a chamber that is just 3 feet (1 m) below the entrance mound. She hears the swooshing of the eagle's wings as it flies away in search of easier prey.

The group returns to the surface. The male flings himself up onto his hind legs. *Wee-oh! Wee-oh!* He throws his head back, yips, and drops to all fours. This is the all-clear signal. He repeats it again and again. Prairie dogs on other mounds in other territories join in. Soon all over the colony, prairie dogs are jumping and yipping.

The noisy chorus is soon over. The prairie dogs go back to eating, working on burrow mounds, and fighting off intruders. Group members also groom one another, tugging out bits of woolly winter undercoat to prepare for the hot summer ahead.

Inside the younger female's nesting chamber, two babies, called pups, are sleeping. When they were born, they were hairless and their eyes were closed. They were not much bigger than a bottle cork. Their mother curled around them at night to keep them warm. She returned to the burrow throughout the day to let them nurse. Now that they're five weeks old, they have their first coat of warm fur. Their mother can leave early in the morning and feed all day. She brings home plants for the pups to eat. She'll also rush home if she spots a predator or another prairie dog approaching her burrow entrance.

When the two pups are about six weeks old, they come out from their nursery burrow. At about the same time, the eight pups of the older female also come to the surface. The pups will hunt for plants, and they'll also continue to nurse. When a pup is hungry, it will nurse from the closest mother. This helps the pups as well as the older female, who has eight pups to feed. Nursing so many pups uses up a lot of her energy. The less she nurses, the more she can use her food to build up a reserve of fat on her body. She will need this fat when snow falls in winter and food becomes scarce.

When they aren't eating or looking for food, the youngsters play. One pup chases another until it's close enough to pounce. Another pup grabs a sibling, and the pair wrestles. Playing helps the pups become stronger. It also helps the pups develop the skills they'll need to escape predators and to defend their group's territory. The young males also learn ways to fight. They'll need fighting skills when they are older. Later, tired of playing, the pups explore their group's territory together. They learn the fastest routes to the burrow's entrances and where to find food.

Chirk! Chirk! Chirk! One evening, alarm calls alert the colony that a black-footed ferret is nearby. The older female and a pack of pups run toward the closest burrow entrance. There the female and the pups stretch up tall, watching for the hunter. But they don't see the ferret right away. Its long, narrow shape blends into the shadows.

The ferret spots a young prairie dog alone at a burrow entrance. Scurrying through the burrow's underground tunnels, the ferret quickly grabs the prairie dog by the neck and holds on tight to make the kill. The ferret drags its prey into the burrow. The ferret's teeth are so sharp that it easily snips through flesh and bones and quickly gulps down its meal. Few scraps are left for beetles and other scavengers.

Another day, a prowling coyote approaches the colony. The cautious prairie dogs sound the alarm, and the coyote goes away hungry.

Early in the summer, the group's young adult male leaves home. Instinctively, he avoids neighboring groups. When young females leave home, they usually move next door. The young male travels far enough away within the colony to avoid mating with his relatives.

The young male has to find a place in another group. This means fighting and chasing out the resident male. The young male yips a challenge. The resident male studies his opponent and waits. Suddenly, the young male attacks. The rivals growl as they wrestle, kicking up dust and struggling to nip each other. The young male darts away, but he soon returns and attacks again.

The opponents leap into the air as they try to pounce on each other. They nip at each other and crash into the dust together. Blood mats the coats of both males.

The young male is agile, quick, and determined. The older male is slower, but he is a more experienced fighter. The battle continues for nearly thirty minutes. The group's females and youngsters watch, chattering noisily. Finally, the older male gives up and leaves. For the next few days, he rests and feeds on the outskirts of his old territory. Then he moves on.

He picks out another group within the colony and battles with the resident male there. When he wins, that group's male moves on, and the process is repeated. If the male is unable to find a home within the colony, he will try to find one in another prairie dog town. A single male is more at risk of being picked out by a predator.

For a few weeks, life in the prairie dog town is peaceful. Then a call signals that a rattlesnake is in the neighborhood. The western diamondback rattlesnake is coiled and ready to catch a prairie dog meal. The prairie dogs forget about their territorial claims as the adults join together to attack the snake. Some of them yip and circle to hold the snake's attention. Others rush in from behind to bite the predator.

The snake strikes, but the prairie dogs are fast. They dart away just in time. When the rattlesnake slithers into one of the burrows, the prairie dogs kick dirt into the tunnel and bury the snake.

As autumn days grow shorter, the prairie grasses turn brown. Gusts of wind scatter the grass seeds. Soon snowflakes swirl and dance in icy gusts. With winter, snow blankets the ground and piles up in drifts. The prairie dogs stay safe and warm inside their burrows. On days when the weather is better, they come out to search for food. They eat tough, dry grass stalks and whatever seeds they can find. Sometimes they are lucky and come across the tasty fruit of a prickly pear cactus. If they don't find any food, the prairie dogs have to depend on their bodies' stored fat reserves for energy and to keep warm.

It's February and the snow has melted a little. Everywhere in the colony, prairie dogs are mating. From early morning to evening, the air is filled with the males' mating calls—low, slow yipping. Battles often break out between rival males. They are trying to claim or keep their territory. They are also fighting for the right to mate with the females.

One of the females in the male's new family group has already mated. Her young babies are developing inside her. She finds mouthfuls of dry grass outside her burrow. She carries them home for fresh bedding material for her nesting chamber.

The fighting and mating are over. The prairie dogs can once more focus on eating and watching out for predators. In a little more than a month, the pregnant females will give birth to the newest members of the prairie dog colony. Then the cycle of life continues—a constant struggle to survive between predators and prey.

Looking Back

- Take another look at the prairie dog on page 12. Why do you think prairie dogs need such big front teeth? To find out, take another look at what prairie dogs bite off and eat on pages 7 and 35.

- Look back at the pictures in the book to see different ways prairie dogs use their front paws and their back feet. Pay special attention to the photos on the following pages: 8, 11, 21, and 33.

- Check out the prairie dogs on page 15. Besides their eyes, ears, and nose, prairie dogs have something else to help them be aware of the world around them. Look closely and you'll see the whiskers that help them "feel" their way through their dark underground burrows.

Glossary

BURROW: a tunnel and any connected chambers that an animal digs. The tunnel and chambers are a safe shelter for the animal and may also be used to raise its young.

BURROW ENTRANCE: the opening through which an animal enters its burrow chambers

NURSING: baby animals feeding on their mother's milk

PREDATOR: an animal that is a hunter

PREY: an animal that a predator catches to eat

SCAVENGERS: animals that feed on dead animals, including prey obtained or killed by a predator

TERRITORY: the area within which a prairie dog group usually searches for food and raises its young

TUNNEL: an entrance to a burrow or any passageway connecting the burrow's underground chambers

Further Information

BOOKS

George, Jean Craighead. *One Day in the Prairie.* New York: Harper Trophy, 1996. This storylike description of the prairie during an approaching storm shows prairie dogs in their natural habitat.

Patent, Dorothy Hinshaw, and William Munoz. *Prairie Dogs.* New York: Clarion, 1993. In addition to information on prairie dog behavior, this book explains reasons the prairie dog population has dramatically decreased.

Winner, Cherie, et al. *Prairie Animals.* Minnetonka, MN: Northword Press, 2004. This is an introduction to the prairie and the animals living there: prairie dogs, bison, hawks, and wild horses.

VIDEO

American Grasslands (Port Royal, SC: Environmental Media Corporation, 2002). This set of six short videos offers a close-up, in-depth look at the unique prairie ecosystem and its wildlife. Recommended by the National Science Teachers Association.

WEBSITES

Save the Prairie Dog
http://www.prairiedogs.org/index.html
Learn about efforts to protect prairie dogs and their homes. If prairie dogs live in your area, click on "How You Can Help."

Underdogs
http://www.nationalgeographic.com/burrow/tb1.html
Dive into a prairie dog burrow with National Geographic to learn more about these animals.

Index

With love for Scott and Heather Markle

The author would like to thank the following people for sharing their expertise and enthusiasm: Dr. John L. Hoogland, Appalachian Laboratory, Center for Environmental Science, University System of Maryland; and Dr. Con Slobodchikoff, Department of Biology, Northern Arizona University. The author would also like to express a special thank-you to Skip Jeffery for his help and support during the creative process.

Photo Acknowledgments

The images in this book are used with the permission of: © D. Robert & Lorri Franz/CORBIS, p. 1; © Rich Kirchner, pp. 3, 11, 17, 23; © Jim Brandenburg/Minden Pictures, pp. 5, 12, 15, 32, 36; © Eastcott Momatiuk/The Image Bank/Getty Images, p. 7; © Tom and Pat Leeson, pp. 8, 9, 13, 33, 35; © W. Perry Conway/CORBIS, p. 19; © Russell Graves, p. 21; © Jeff Vanuga/Vanuga Photography, pp. 24, 25; © Lynn M. Stone, p. 26; © Jeff Foott/Bruce Coleman, Inc., p. 27; © Raymond K. Gehman/National Geographic/Getty Images, p. 29; © Tom Lazar/www.LazarArt.com, p. 31; © Wendy Shattil and Bob Rozinski/Oxford Scientific Films, p. 37. Cover: © W. Perry Conway/CORBIS.

Lerner Publications Company
A division of Lerner Publishing Group
241 First Avenue North
Minneapolis, MN 55401 U.S.A.

Website address: www.lernerbooks.com

Library of Congress Cataloging-in-Publication Data

Markle, Sandra.
  Prairie dogs / by Sandra Markle.
    p.   cm. — (Animal prey)
  Includes bibliographical references and index.
  ISBN-13: 978−0−8225−6438−6 (lib. bdg. : alk. paper)
  ISBN-10: 0−8225−6438−6 (lib. bdg. : alk. paper)
  1. Prairie dogs—Juvenile literature. I. Title. II. Series: Markle, Sandra. Animal prey.
QL737.R68M3317 2007
599.36'7—dc22   2006000598

Manufactured in the United States of America
1 2 3 4 5 6 − DP − 12 11 10 09 08 07